My Many Miracles:

"A Spiritual Journey"

My Many Miracles:

"A Spiritual Journey"

Eugene F. Elander

LANG
BOOK PUBLISHING

LANG
BOOK PUBLISHING

langbookpublishing.com

National Library of New Zealand Cataloguing-in-Publication Data.

Lang Book Publishing 2018.

ISBN 978-1-9885571-7-5 – Softback
ISBN 978-0-9951045-0-1 – Hardback
ISBN 978-0-9941291-4-7 – eBook

Published in New Zealand.

A catalogue record for this book is available from the National Library of New Zealand.

Kei te pātengi raraunga o Te Puna Mātauranga o Aotearoa te whakarārangi o tēnei pukapuka.

So Many Miracles

So many miracles, life does comprise,
As we would see, had we only the eyes;
So many miracles, with smiles or tears,
As we would hear, had we only the ears;
So many miracles, which truly are real,
As we would touch, had we only the feel;
So many miracles, with faith playing its part,
As we would know, had we only the heart.

There are more things in heaven and earth, Horatio,
Than are dreamt of in your philosophy.

Hamlet, by William Shakespeare, Hamlet to Horatio,
(1,5. 167-8)

TABLE OF CONTENTS

FOREWORD

I did not write this book; rather, this book wrote me. The manner in which both the concept and content came to me seems, in and of itself, a bit of a miracle. But, that is getting ahead of the story. So, let me begin at the beginning.

It seems to me that there is a fundamental truth about miracles. Their very nature has changed and evolved with the evolution of humanity, but they are still present in our lives, if only we can recognize them. This realization came upon me rather gradually, stemming from a series of events which seemed unexplainable by any ordinary means. It is those events which are described in this book, along with some interpretation as to why they may well be considered miraculous in nature. Miracles, like truth and beauty, lie in the eye, and mind, of the beholder. And, like truth and beauty, I consider that miracles do, in fact, occur and exist.

Of course, skeptics will attribute these same events to so-called natural causes, or perhaps even deny their existence. As to causation, that is left to the reader – but I can and do assert with full assurance that the descriptions which follow are truthful and complete, to the best of my recollection. These events have taken place in my life – they are actual occurrences.

The further contention, and hope, of this book, is that the reader will be guided to find miracles in his or her own life. Perhaps some of those miracles were not recognized when they occurred, but were noted later. Perhaps others were never recognized at all.

It would be truly sad to live a life without miracles, or to not find those which occurred.

As to the source or sources of miracles, those determinations are also left to the reader. It would be very presumptuous for this author to speculate on the religious aspects of our miracles, beyond the Afterword in this book. Suffice it to say that, by finding our own miracles, studying them, and trying to understand their sources for ourselves, our personal spiritual journeys can be immensely enhanced. There is much to ponder in this book, but much more to ponder in your own life. May your miracles be many, and may you find them a source of true enlightenment.

INTRODUCTION:
ON THE NATURE OF MIRACLES

How does one determine whether a particular event, occurrence, or thing represents a miracle? Of course, one must believe in the possibility of miracles in order for any such determination to make sense. This book takes, as a given, that miracles are not only possible, but indeed that they occur more often than is commonly believed.

The reasons for such disbelief may have more to do with this skeptical age than with the nature of miracles themselves. Although many of the world's greatest scientists, such as Albert Einstein, have been intensely spiritual persons, and although so many people still seek spiritual truths and enlightenment, the fact remains that in the Western World, we are less swayed by the unexplained and unexplainable than was the case for past generations.

It is the contention of this book that there is a further reason for the present skepticism about miracles. The nature of miracles itself has changed and evolved over the millennia.

Whether Moses persuaded the Almighty to part the Red (or Reed) Sea so as to let the Hebrews escape the army of the Egyptian Pharaoh several thousand years ago remains open to debate. Whether the miracles attributed to Jesus and some of his followers really constitute fact or fiction is more a matter of faith and belief than of firm historical events.

Whether the miracles required of those being named saints have been actual events, or rather were contrived after the fact to justify their sainthood, remains disputed territory.

Perhaps, then, we must search elsewhere for the miracles of today. In order to conduct such a search intelligently, we must first define what we mean by the term 'miracle' itself.

This book poses four requirements for some event, occurrence, or thing to be considered miraculous in nature: First, it must be unexplainable by normal, rational considerations. Second, it must be considered positive in nature by the person who is experiencing it. Third, the proposed miracle must be personal in nature; it must have occurred directly to a specific person or persons. Finally, it must be significant and substantive, as determined largely by the person(s) experiencing the alleged miracle.

The miracles described in this book meet all four of these criteria, based on the judgment of the author. Each reader is of course welcome to make his or her own determination as to the nature and source of these occurrences. At least try to keep an open mind. If you are encouraged to seek your own miracles after reading these, that is sufficient.

ONE

THE FORTUITOUS FALL

Autumn, 1954
Jamaica, Queens, New York

Preamble

It may seem strange that My Many Miracles begins with an event related to falling, in the physical sense, and contains another miracle based on the fear of falling off a mountain. (Section Three.) A key reason for the significance of falling seems to stem from the many meanings of the term in common English usage: falling in love, falling for a financial scheme, the falling rain or snow, even the fall of man – the list is endless. From this list, one can see that, indeed, falling may be good or bad, useful or useless, beneficial or harmful – but, nearly always, falling is impactful. My first miracle resulted from what turned out to be a most beneficial fall, for my future – a case of falling which ultimately has led to this very book; here, then, is the tale of my first miracle.

* * *

For as long as I can remember, I have always wished to be smart. When other children my age wanted to be major league baseball players, or movie stars, or cops, or even war heroes (World War II had just ended), I wanted to be a 'brain', as smart kids were called during that era. I was a skinny, un-athletic, shy child. In my third grade classroom at P.S. 82 in Jamaica, Queens, New York, I envied those kids who sat at the front of the class and always seemed to have the right answers. While I was not dumb, I was only a mediocre student at best, and all of my efforts at studying and reading seemed to have little effect on that reality.

Perhaps my focus on intelligence emanated from the stereotypical American Jewish family which was then depicted in radio shows, newspapers, and magazines. Perhaps it stemmed from being an only child who was usually treated as an adult by his parents. The classic story about that type of background involved a grade-schooler who came home boasting of getting a score of 98 in math, only to have his mother respond: "So, who got the other two points?"

Being named for my great-grand-uncle Ulich, who had been a distinguished physician in Warsaw, Poland and had even treated the last Russian Czar, my family assumed that I would go on to become a doctor. But I knew better. I did not have the brains for a medical career, yet I prayed that I might become smarter.

One weekday in the autumn of 1945, my mother Anne sent me to get a few groceries at a neighborhood store on Jamaica Avenue. This was one of my frequent after-school duties. Usually I would just put the change from the cash transaction in my pocket, but for some reason I decided to count that change as I walked home that day. Perhaps I thought that the grocer had made a mistake. In any event, I was not watching out for the metal plates, which most stores had out in front, covering the steps to their basements where goods were stored.

Suddenly, only a few stores down from the grocery store, my feet came out from under me and I was falling through the air as the change from the store flew out of my hand.

I had fallen through an open set of horizontal metal plates and down a ten-foot flight of steps, into the basement of another store and landed hard on the top of my head. I felt a sharp pain, and then nothing more until I awoke on a bed in the emergency room at Jamaica Hospital, where the fire department rescue team had taken me from that store basement after I appeared unresponsive. I was diagnosed with a concussion, kept for several hours for observation, and then sent home with my very worried parents, who had been called by the fire department, based on information from neighborhood merchants.

I was kept home from school for the next few days, after a follow-up appointment with Dr. Kaufmann, our family physician. During that respite, I studied my upcoming lessons, and suddenly found them much more understandable than they had been before my fall. Now I could carry out long division and other arithmetic operations with ease. My penmanship had also improved and my reading skills seemed enhanced. Strangest of all, a speech impediment which I had displayed, involving pronouncing the letter R as a W, which made me the butt of classroom jokes related to Bugs Bunny cartoons, seemed to be gone. I no longer needed to recite, over and over, 'Round and Round the Rugged Rock the Ragged Rascal Ran' – an exercise I had been given to help my pronunciation. I seemed to be cured, and I surprised my parents with my newfound competence with the letter R.

It took the remainder of that autumn for my parents to notice my improved schoolwork and grades. When they asked me about those gains, I had no explanation, but they noted that everything had begun with my fall down the store steps. Somehow, it seemed, my brain had been re-wired more effectively as a result of that fall. Dr. Kaufmann was asked about that during my final check-up a month later, and he stated unequivocally that there was no medical explanation for my improvement in school – falling down a flight of steps never made anyone the slightest bit smarter, according to the good doctor.

Nevertheless, after that pivotal fall, I was skipped twice in school, placing me a full year ahead of my former classmates, so that I graduated from the eighth grade at twelve years of age. Two years later, in 1950, we moved from New York City to South Dayton (now Kettering), Ohio. I graduated from Fairmont High School there at age sixteen, after scoring fifth in the entire State on the Ohio High School statewide regents-type exam. I then went off to study electrical engineering at MIT, after also being admitted to both the Harvard and Brown Ivy League universities. I had indeed become smart. My early prayers had been answered, and this was my first miracle! It would turn out to be far from the last…

TWO
A BREAK REGARDING
THE BRAKES

July, 1954
Richmond, Indiana

Preamble

My father Martin taught me to drive during the summer of 1953, a bit before I turned sixteen years of age in late August of that year and could take my driving test. Our family had flown from Dayton, Ohio to Los Angeles for a tour of Southern California. Dad's company, United Aircraft Products, had a West Coast office, which had a company car – a 1952 Chrysler semi-automatic. This meant that instead of shifting gears, you had to let up on the gas to go into the next higher gear – a system that worked quite well. I became a reasonably-competent, if not yet legal, driver that summer, and took my driving test on my sixteenth birthday, with the motor vehicle driving inspector saying sarcastically that I had to be a fast learner since I had only obtained my learner's permit that same day.

My parents had told me that if I wanted to have my own car, I would have to pay for it with money earned during the summer, and I had worked as a clothing sales associate at the local J.C. Penny store to do so. That summer, before we all left for the West Coast, I had picked out a 1940 Chevy Coupe priced at two hundred dollars at a local used car dealer. This became my pride and joy. After removing the running boards from below both doors, cleaning up and waxing the car, and of course adding a pair of large fuzzy dice to hang from the rear view mirror, I was ready for an adventure, once my license was secured. Relishing my newfound freedom, each weekend became a driving event throughout the region. This tale relates to one driving event which nearly cost me life or limb, were it not for a well-timed miracle – here, then, was my second miracle.

* * *

It was the start of a warm summer weekend in July, 1954, and I was playing a game of Random Choice on my Gulf Gas map of Ohio, Indiana, and Kentucky. I would close my eyes and jab an index finger at the map, then drive to wherever my finger chose. These solo jaunts were aided by my father letting me use his company gasoline card – since he was the company treasurer, this was no problem. One Saturday, my finger landed near Angola, Indiana, with its nearby State park, an underground river, and excellent camping.

Heading off to Indiana, about forty miles West of Dayton, Ohio, I took old Route 40, then called National Highway as it crossed much of America – now upgraded as Interstate 70. I went North on Route 35 at Richmond, Indiana, and headed towards Angola, which was several hours away. About halfway there, I saw steam coming out of the front of my old Chevy, which, in the days before car radiators had storage tanks, meant that it was overheating. Luckily – or so I thought – there was a nearby gas station along Route 35, and I pulled in to let the radiator cool down so that I could check for the source of the problem and then add water as needed. This was a common summer experience with older cars in those days.

Since I also needed gasoline, I had pulled into the lane by the gas pumps, and then made a quick trip to the rest room since there were no other vehicles waiting for gas there. Just as I returned to the gas pumps, I saw that my hood had been raised – and I heard a loud crack coming from the front of the car. Running the rest of the way, I found the gas station attendant pouring a pail of cold water into my overheated radiator and engine. The loud crack was not a good sign, as every teenager in Ohio, and most adults, knew. One should never pour cold water into a hot radiator or engine as the motor head and block are likely to be cracked by the sudden metal contraction. That is often fatal.

The owner of the gas station, who turned out to be the father of the attendant, also heard the cracking sound, and came out of the office to investigate. Shaking his head sadly, the owner apologized profusely for the negligence of his son, but immediately proposed a solution: coincidentally, he had a car available to swap for my Chevy, and because his son was at fault, they would make an 'even-steven swap', as it was called. So in exchange for my injured but otherwise pristine 1940 Chevy, I was offered a 1941 Pontiac, which seemed decent, at least from the outside. Since my Chevy appeared to be un-driveable due to serious engine damage, I had little choice in the matter. Of course, the titles for both cars would have to be exchanged later, since I was not old enough to have them in my name, but that could be done through the mail if necessary. I test drove the Pontiac. It had a lovely combination of black paint and light rust with yellow fog lights and a metal sunshade. I then headed back home, instead of Angola.

My priorities for the day had changed, as had my vehicle, and I just hoped to get back to Dayton safe and sound.

I had been driving for about an hour, during which I noted that the brakes on the old Pontiac were a bit squishy and had to be pumped in order to stop – not unusual with old cars.

In this time, I had returned to the biggest intersection in Richmond, Indiana, where four-lane Routes 40 and 35 came together with many large, slow trucks in the right-hand lane of Route 40. Since I was now heading South on Route 35, intending to turn left onto Route 40 and head home, I was approaching this major intersection in the left-hand lane, when the traffic light changed to yellow, and then to red: STOP. That was when my car's brakes, probably losing the rest of the vital hydraulic fluid which made them work, went out entirely, just as a big semi-trailer truck was crossing my intersection on the green light. I pulled on the hand brake, which I had not checked before, and the handle came off in my hand! I had no brakes at all, and was heading right into the path of the gigantic truck crossing the intersection right in front of me! I heard the blaring of the truck air horn, as time seemed to slow down while my life went reeling before my eyes: it seemed likely to end there and then. Only a miracle could save me!

At that moment – as I rolled into the intersection in front of the truck – I saw a long gravel driveway to my right. I twisted the steering wheel as far as it would go and coasted into the driveway just in time, rolling and bumping along it until the car stopped. The life-saving driveway was slightly uphill, which helped me to stop. I had coasted into an empty wooden one-car garage at the end, which miraculously had an open door.

The Pontiac was only a couple of feet from the cement back wall of the garage, but it was blessedly no longer moving, and neither was I. I sat frozen in the driver's seat. Then I heard a dog barking, and the next thing I saw was a middle-aged man standing behind the car just outside the garage, pointing a shotgun at me and asking me 'What the Hell I Was Doing In His Garage'. When I explained that my brakes had gone out suddenly, he put down the shotgun and told me that there was a truck stop with 24-hour repair service just beyond the Route 40 side of the intersection, and if I drove very carefully on the shoulder of the highway, I should get there safely and they would check my brakes and try to fix them. His advice was taken – and a rusted and leaking brake line was found by the mechanic on-duty, and replaced. Within an hour, I was again on my way home – safely.

The outcome of this entire event was that my father, after making several rather sarcastic remarks about the Pontiac that I had inadvertently acquired, told me that he wanted my old Chevy back. If necessary, the engine could be repaired if it had really been damaged. The next day, we drove back to the Indiana gas station which had the Chevy, and – lo and behold – there was a FOR SALE sign on my original car. The station owner, looking a mite chagrined, said they had discovered that it just needed water (the engine cracking noise was never explained).

My father pointed out that since I was underage, the car swap was not legal. He was quite forceful, even mentioning calling the local sheriff, and we got rid of the Pontiac there and then and drove back home in my old Chevy. We stopped for a meal at the same truck stop which had fixed the brakes on the Pontiac. My father's lecture all the way home was well-deserved. Still, I gave a prayer of thanks as we passed the now-notable driveway – but silently, as I had not mentioned that part of the story. This, indeed, turned out to be my second miracle, and likely a life-saving one at that.

THREE

THE MOUNTAIN
AND ITS SHEEP

August, 1955
Banff, Alberta, Canada

Preamble

At seventeen years of age, while studying Electrical Engineering at MIT, I was still an Explorer Scout and spent
summers with my family in South Dayton, Ohio (now
renamed Kettering in honor of Charles Kettering, the
automotive pioneer who invented the self-starter). My
family and I had moved from Jamaica, New York four
years earlier, in the middle of my high school days, when
my father was promoted to sales manager at his company,
United Aircraft Products, based in Dayton, Ohio. At my
new Fairmont High School, a local Explorer Scout troop
had invited me to join them since I had been an active
Boy Scout in Jamaica. This was a great way to make new
friends in a new town.

After several years of Explorer activities, ranging from
sports to area camping trips, our Scoutmaster, Robert W.
Kuhns, Jr. – known to all as Bob Kuhns – said we were
ready for some serious mountain climbing in the Canadian

Rockies. We had been practicing cliff climbing in Southeastern Ohio, and I felt far from ready for anything more strenuous, but I absolutely did not want to be left behind. There was room for four of us Explorers in Bob's spacious new Chrysler Imperial car and I was determined to occupy one of those spots, even if it killed me – which, as things turned out, it very nearly did.

Bob Kuhns was a unique character. He was a man who had never admitted uncertainty about anything. He had served as a Naval officer in the Pacific Theatre during World War II. We never tired of hearing his stories of how the U.S. Navy evicted invading Japanese from one Pacific island after another, but only at great cost in both lives and armaments. Bob came from a very wealthy family who lived in a mansion in Oakwood, Ohio. Their Kuhns Brothers Foundry produced all sorts of plumbing items, such as pipe-fittings, sold throughout the U.S. and Canada. Bob was a determined bachelor. My family had tried to introduce him to some eligible young women at my father's company, but all such efforts were in vain. Our Explorer Scout troop was his major outside interest, and mountain climbing was an active avocation. Therefore, participation in climbing was mandatory – even for the severely unskilled, like me.

Bob had a required climbing outfit. It consisted of a T-shirt, preferably white, a pair of khaki shorts, long and thick white cotton socks, and a brand of moccasin with an Indian head on the sole. By the start of August 1955, my summer work as a technician in the Test Lab at my father's company was over and I was ready to head off for several weeks of camping and serious, if very scary, mountain climbing! The strangest event occurred on a mountain in Banff, Alberta, Canada – here, then, is the tale of my third miracle:

* * *

Most of our journey to the Canadian Rockies was un-eventful. We camped along the way, while Bob Kuhns visited several distributors of his company's plumbing products. By the time we had reached Banff, we were eager for some real climbing. To tell the full truth, though, my companions were considerably more eager than I was. Rather, I had become increasingly nervous about the pos-sibility of falling off a mountain. Still, we had practiced on several American peaks in Colorado and Utah, and the worst problem I had experienced was bringing up the rear of our little group. I may have been slow, but I was at least a steady climber, even without any real equipment – a part of the challenge!

We camped along Lake Louise, a beautiful body of green water near the quaint town of Banff, then not yet a tourist trap. The next morning, in mid-August of 1955, we began our ascent of the mountain overlooking Lake Louise. The first part of the climb was on shale and broken rock, and I began to lag behind. For a while, my friends waited for me to catch up, but I told them to go ahead as I did not want to delay them. Also, to be honest, I had a game plan: I would get as high on the mountain as seemed practical for me and then turn back discreetly. This was a tactic which I had used on some previous climbs, but it came with the disadvantage of being alone on the mountain – a situation really most unwise for climbers.

By noon, I managed to get about halfway up the mountain, stopping to eat an orange for lunch on a narrow ledge high above the now-tiny lake. After finishing the orange, I made the mistake of throwing the peel over the edge of the ledge, and the even greater mistake of watching it fall several thousand feet. Suddenly, having gotten onto my feet, I had a sense of vertigo and hugged the rough stone of the mountain above the ledge – when, to my extreme surprise, a bighorn mountain sheep came around the corner of the ledge, appearing suddenly from higher up on the mountain. This was the first mountain sheep I had ever seen, and it did not appear overly friendly or eager to make my acquaintance. Nor was I eager to get to know the mountain sheep any better, or to have it get any closer.

The problem, however, was that there was no room for both of us to pass on the narrow ledge, and the sheep and I were heading in opposite directions. As my first shock began to diminish a bit, I thought of a simple cure for part of the problem: I would begin my descent of the mountain at once. Then, I realized that the mountain sheep could descend much faster than I could, and would therefore still try to pass me on the ledge. I could not ascend either, as that would force me to try to pass the sheep, whose horns alone were nearly the width of the ledge. The situation, therefore, seemed to offer no resolution in my favor.

While I was not known for my religious fervor at that time – nor, for that matter, ever since – it seemed to me that praying could not hurt in this seemingly-impossible situation. Further motivating my prayers was the mountain sheep's lowering of its horned head as if preparing to charge me. Therefore, I prayed that, being only seventeen years old and having my entire life in front of me, I would greatly appreciate an opportunity to live that life, and would do my best to accomplish some useful things if that opportunity were to be granted. I addressed this prayer to whomsoever might help me.

Meanwhile, while praying, I kept a wary eye on my opponent-on-the-ledge. Up until then, the mountain sheep and I had not really made eye contact. Now, however, I felt that the animal was staring at me, perhaps preparing to butt me off the ledge so that I could follow the orange peel down to destruction. Instead, though, the sheep stared me in the face for a long moment – and then turned around carefully on the narrow ledge and went back the way it had come, back up the mountain. I was saved by what I later came to call 'The Miracle of the Mountain'.

Having no desire to follow the mountain sheep onwards and upwards, I turned tail and went slowly back down the mountain, then waited at the base for my colleagues to return. They appeared unsurprised that I had not made it to the top. They confessed that the climb was quite difficult – Bob Kuhns even commented that there were other mountains; and indeed, further up in the Canadian Rockies, after the Columbia Icefields, I did climb a peak near Jasper. On the long ride back to Dayton, Ohio, after our camping trip, when asked about what happened near Banff, I started to talk about the experience with the mountain sheep – leading to some unkind remarks from my colleagues. So, I let the tale remain untold for many years.

I can only conclude that, while the mountain sheep may have had my front, someone or some power had my back on that memorable day in August 1955. For that I will always be thankful and grateful. Nor have I forgotten my vow to lead a useful life afterwards.

That was the third of my many miracles which I can clearly recall – a miracle whose life-saving result perhaps also showed the power of prayer.

FOUR
THE VISION

Spring, 1969
Brigantine, New Jersey

Preamble

On December 7, 1962, while I was in my third year of graduate school in Economics at the University of Pennsylvania in Philadelphia, the phone in my small rented room rang suddenly, after one o'clock in the morning. Such late night or early morning calls rarely bring good news, and this one was no exception. Our family attorney, Asher Bogin, was calling to inform me with deep regret that my father, Martin Elander, had died suddenly of a heart attack while at Miami Valley Hospital in Dayton, Ohio. He had gone for tests that the family had thought to be routine. Martin was fifty-six years of age, and there had been no signs of major health problems, except for diabetes, which was under control – but he had been complaining of not feeling well since Thanksgiving, so our family MD Kenneth Arn had sent him for tests.

The last time I saw my father was over that Thanksgiving; he and I had driven to Dayton from Philadelphia. He had taken the train to Philadelphia from his monthly company Board Meeting in New York. This was a trek we made several times each year so that we could spend some time together, sharing the 800-mile drive to the Ohio family home. I noticed on this trip that his driving seemed a bit erratic and asked him if everything was all right; he replied that he was just tired. Apparently, it was considerably more than that. At least we got to spend his last Thanksgiving together, with my mother too, as a family. Unfortunately, it became the final occasion when that would be possible.

One of the hardest things I can recall about that period was picking up Dad's personal items at the hospital; the staff seemed cold and callous, and nobody even expressed regret over his demise. I suspected that Miami Valley Hospital had done something wrong to cause that demise, and later learned that he had been given some medication that had loosened a blood clot in his leg and sent it to block an artery into his heart. But, in those days, filing a malpractice suit was much less common than it is today, and perhaps would not have been justified. Regardless of the circumstances, my father was now gone forever.

My mother and I made funeral arrangements for Martin in Forest Hills, New York. Dad's burial was to be in the New Mount Carmel cemetery in Woodhaven, New York, where there was an Elander family plot. His company, United Aircraft Products, put us up at Manhattan's Essex House to wait for the funeral and burial. Mother then returned to Dayton while I went back to the University of Pennsylvania to complete that semester.

To tell the truth, though, my mind was not much on my final exams in December 1962.

I had become very angry over the unexpected loss of Martin at such an early age. We had had wonderful times together as a family: seeing Cincinnati Reds baseball games and University of Dayton basketball games together, sharing annual trips to Miami over the Winter holidays, taking a memorable National Parks vacation including the 1961 Seattle World Fair, and so many other activities which would never, ever be the same again. I was, and remained, quite bitter, feeling that life had indeed let me down.

I had not realized how dependent I still was on my father, even after leaving home for graduate school in Philadelphia. In my mid-twenties, I had never even thought of losing him to a heart attack or anything else. At that age, life seems eternal – until we learn better. Then, seven years later, I learned a perhaps-miraculous lesson – here is the tale of my fourth miracle:

* * *

By the Spring of 1969, I had assumed a new position at a new institution. Atlantic Community College, near Atlantic City, New Jersey, had offered me the chairmanship of its fledgling Business Administration and Economics Division, along with an Associate Professorship. The offer was too good to refuse, and my family and I had piled into our old 1957 Chevy Wagon over the Summer of 1968 and driven straight through from Ohio to our new home in Brigantine, New Jersey, the next island North of Atlantic City.

As we settled into life at the charming South Jersey shore, I settled into the routine of a new college department head: hiring faculty, developing curriculum, resolving problems, steering my unit through its initial accreditation, and also teaching three courses each semester. All of that work, plus adjusting to a very different lifestyle from that which came with teaching in Ohio, tended to leave me very tired most evenings. By the time I would fall asleep, I did not dream much, nor could I recall any dreams the next morning. However, all of that changed one Spring night in 1969.

As I lay sleeping, a strange dream came to me – more of a vision, really, as it was in full color and great detail. I saw my father, Martin, wearing a brownish patterned suit, but looking much younger than I remembered him. He was puttering around our old apartment in Jamaica, New York, from which we had moved to Ohio in the early 1950s.

I seemed to be watching him, and he said something like 'I am fine' to me. Then, I awoke.

This strange dream or vision haunted me for the next few days, until the weekend came, and I drove up to Rego Park, New York for a monthly visit with my mother Anne, who had moved there from Ohio in order to be near her sister Esther in Jamaica and brother Harry in Forest Hills (my mother did not drive, and living in Ohio required a car, which also encouraged her to move back to the New York City area). After our usual greetings, I told my mother that I had had a strange dream, which I described to her in as much detail as I could recall. There was a long pause after I had finished. I awaited her reply.

Noting that my mother looked troubled, I asked her what was wrong. She paused again and then told me that she recalled the suit my father was wearing in my dream, but that it dated back to their early years of marriage, in the 1930s, when he was selling cars after losing his office job with their company, American Metals Climax, due to the depression. She said his sales manager had told him that he had to wear a salesman's suit, and he had purchased a brown check model – but had never liked it – and when he got a hernia from pushing a car, he found another job, and got rid of that suit. Mother concluded that I had never seen that suit, and there were no photos of my father in it since he had disliked it so much. Neither of us could understand how I had seen or imagined him in it, particularly as I only recalled him in solid or striped fabrics in real life. We puzzled over the dream or vision for the rest of that visit together, and afterwards too.

Whatever had happened regarding such a strange event – wishful thinking or some kind of real vision – remains unexplained to this day. Still, I remain convinced that my father had gotten a message to me, causing my bitterness over his untimely demise to gradually diminish. In its place, eventually, came the recognition that life has no guarantees as to either length or content, and all of us must make the most of the time that we have. It was a lesson well-learned, and was also my fourth miracle.

FIVE

THE HURRICANE

September 9, 1969
Brigantine, New Jersey

Preamble

Hurricane Gerda, according to official weather reports, was a major North Atlantic tropical storm that formed during the 1969 Atlantic hurricane season. It was the seventh named storm, fifth hurricane, and third major hurricane of the 1969 season. Gerda formed offshore on September 6 and first crossed Florida as a serious tropical depression, then later becoming a tropical storm after making a hard right turn, moving northeast, and reaching hurricane status on September 8. The next day, Gerda reached the maximum wind intensity of 125 mph (205 km/h) and a low barometric pressure of 979 millibars (28.9 in Hg) while moving up the Atlantic coastline, even passing the State of New Jersey that evening. On September 10, Gerda made landfall near Eastport, Maine, and then headed out to sea. Here is my own tale of a miraculous Hurricane Gerda event, which may be considered as my fifth miracle:

* * *

When we purchased our home in Brigantine, New Jersey, shortly after I was offered the chair of the Business and Economics Division at nearby Atlantic Community College in 1968, we were also fulfilling a major dream: to live along the shore on the Atlantic coast.

Our home at 838 West Shore Drive was directly on the Inland Waterway, between the island of Brigantine and the New Jersey coastline, just North of Atlantic City. Our ranch-style house has been built by a local contractor a few years earlier, and the builder had lived in the house until he sold it to us – along with an old sixteen-foot mahogany boat, sitting on a boat trailer in the front yard.

After doing some renovations to the boat, which was re-named as the John B, taken from the folk song about a ship of that same name, I had a mooring pole sunk in the waterway right behind our bulkhead, so that the front of the John B could be tied to the new pole, while the rear of our boat was secured by two ropes to heavy metal rings set in the wooden bulkhead behind our house. Although I knew nothing about boats, and even less about fastening them down, I had seen similar arrangements used to secure other small boats along the Waterway. Since we were not located on the Atlantic itself, the waves were usually gentle; and the water was deep enough to handle even low tides, so the mooring seemed safe and secure. That is, until Hurricane Gerda came along the following Autumn, to test that mooring, and to test me as well. Here is what happened, to me and to the John B, on that fateful evening of September 9, 1969:

As winds started rising on September 9, 1969, I had been working in my office at Atlantic Community College, while listening to local radio reports warning of the incipient hurricane heading up the coast towards Atlantic City and environs. People in that area tended to take tropical storms and even hurricanes in their stride as they had seen many such events, including the destruction of the famed Atlantic City Boardwalk years before, and still survived.

Nevertheless, I headed home in mid-afternoon to check on our house, its property, and of course the John B, moored behind the house. All seemed well, aside from the rising shriek of the wind, and the difficulty driving across the bridge to Brigantine Island as my heavy Cadillac convertible became hard to steer safely. Making it home, I began securing all the loose objects that were in the yard and attached to the house. I then went to our bulkhead in the back to check on the John B. I tightened up all mooring lines and finally went inside as the wind continued to rise. Meanwhile, news reports on television warned of severe hurricane risks.

At about nine in the evening, with the wind rising, I decided to go out back again, to the bulkhead, to see how the John B was doing – only to find that it was not doing so well. One of the two rear mooring lines had come loose from its ring, and the other rear line seemed insecure too. As I watched, that second line broke at the ring, but I managed to grab hold of it before the rear of our boat swung out into the now-very-strong current of the Waterway. While holding that rear line tight, I wondered what I could do next, as trying to re-secure it was hopeless. Since I could not figure out any real course of action, I had to just hang onto that rope with my full weight, leaning against the still-rising wind, and hoping against hope that the final rope, in front, did not break or come loose, as there was no way I could reach that remaining rope in time and then the John B. would be lost.

After about three hours of holding on for dear life with that rope wrapped around my arm – while watching some very nice boats come down the Waterway with nobody on board, spinning around in the current, and sometimes hitting the opposite shore across from our house – a New Jersey Coast Guard vessel came down the Waterway, and an officer with a bull horn yelled at me to get back inside the house. His comments were far from polite, starting with: "What the hell is wrong with you!? Get inside – right now!"

I tried to shout back that I was saving my small boat – and I will never know whether or not he heard me, as the Coast Guard vessel continued struggling down the Waterway, while I continued to pull on that mooring rope with all the strength I had left. I also began to say some prayers at that point, particularly since the sandy soil in our backyard was eroding under my feet and I was sliding towards the nearby back bulkhead at an angle. If that slide continued, the John B. was likely to become the least of my problems, as I would probably go right over into the rushing water and be carried away myself. Now, the wind and rain had become so strong that it was unlikely that I could make it back to the house, should I decide to let go of the rope. Since there were no good options, all I could do was to hold on – and continue to pray! I found that I was also becoming angry: what right did this hurricane have to take away our boat, or to send me into the foaming water? No way! I vowed to never give up and never give in to the storm!

After what seemed like an eternity, but was actually about six hours, the winds began to taper off and the pressure on the rope, which I was still holding, began to diminish. Since I did not know if this was the result of being in the eye of the hurricane, so that the wind would rise again shortly, I continued to hold onto the mooring line. At least my feet were no longer slipping. After about a half hour, I decided the worst of Hurricane Gerda was over, and I was able to re-fasten the mooring line which I was holding. The second line had come loose and was drifting in the water. I could grab hold of its end. My Scout training came in handy, by helping me to use the best knots for this purpose, until all three mooring lines could be replaced, on a calm day.

As morning light began to show through the heavy cloud cover, I went inside the house for a much-needed cup of coffee – and sat down stiffly, finding that my legs preferred not to bend while my hands were severely chapped. Every muscle in my body seemed sore, and I debated going to the emergency room for a checkup – but since my college was closed due to the weather, I just went to bed instead and slept nearly around the clock.

Hurricane Gerda meanwhile headed on up towards New England. The John B. was full of rain water, but otherwise safe and sound, unlike so many larger boats which were lost in that hurricane. The next week, when I spoke about these events, experienced sailors in the Brigantine Jaycees group of which I was an officer expressed disbelief that a boat could be saved after two of its three mooring lines had come loose. John Rizzo, our realtor and a fellow Jaycee, commented that it would take a miracle to save any boat moored so poorly and insecurely by an inexperienced boat owner in a hurricane. He was most probably right; and, thus, this was my fifth miracle.

SIX
THE CAR BOMBING

October 28, 1973
UN Plaza, New York City

Preamble

Terrorism in the 1970s and early 1980s took very different forms from those of such despicable activity today. Then, there were weaponed attacks in Northern Ireland on English police officers and officials, by the fearsome Irish Republican Army. There were pocket bombs placed inside Canadian postal boxes by Quebec separatists, sometimes resulting in mailmen having their arms blown off. There were anti-Soviet terror tactics, such as attacks on diplomats by the Jewish Defense League over the Soviet refusal to release some of its Jewish population to go to Israel or America. There were American terror groups, such as the Weathermen and the Black Panthers, with their own agendas and a willingness to promote violence in order to achieve those agendas.

And there were several Armenian terrorist units, including the Armenian Secret Army, which engaged in bombings of Turkish facilities around the world and assassinated some Turkish diplomats over the early 20th

Century Armenian Genocide by the Turkish Ottoman Empire and Turkey's ongoing refusal to provide for an Armenian homeland. This is the true tale of how I was saved from the drastic results of one such terror attack by a seemingly-miraculous event, my sixth miracle of note:

* * *

On Saturday, October 6, 1973, the Day of Atonement and holiest day of the year for those of the Jewish faith, including most Israelis, the leading Arab nations combined forces in a sneak attack on the State of Israel, even as devout prayers were underway.

Perhaps, in part, as a result of those prayers, Israel not only survived, but won the war, which became known as the Yom Kippur War. Still, the cost in Israeli lives and property damage was overwhelming, and supporters of Israel all over the world pitched in with vital resources to assist in the restoration of normality to Israel, even as the war ended.

On Friday, October 26, 1973, some four hundred pro-Israel leaders from all over North America met at the B'nai B'rith Building at United Nations Plaza in Manhattan. Since I was executive director of an agency in New London, Connecticut, which both raised funds and promoted the positive aspects of the fledgling State of Israel, and since I also served on a national community relations commission focusing on related issues, I drove down from home early that morning, arriving in mid-town New York just after the conference had started. I parked a few blocks away on First Avenue, just off the East River, and walked to the conference location. Following an assembly-type meeting, we broke into smaller groups to discuss the various issues related to the Yom Kippur War and Israel.

The focus of my group was to provide accurate, supportive facts to our communities, and to the general public, about how the recent War would likely affect Israeli-U.S. relations.

The conference was scheduled to end at 5 p.m., in order to allow local people time to get home before the start of the Sabbath. For some unexplained reason, though, I began to get nervous some minutes before 5 p.m., as if I were pressured with a clear message to leave the meeting a bit early. This feeling grew and grew, until at around 4:50 p.m. I abruptly got up from my chair and left, not even stopping at the bathroom down the hall first. A few people stared as I left, as it must have appeared quite rude to rush off while such a major meeting was still underway. But by then, the pressure on me to leave had become a compulsion.

As I walked from the B'nai B'rith building and headed along UN Plaza, towards my parking lot, I noticed an older-model American car parked with two wheels on the sidewalk right outside an office which had letters on its glass front identifying it as the Turkish Information Office at 821 United Nations Plaza. I shook my head, muttering about New Yorkers who park any way they wish, ignoring many parking tickets until they just change cars and start all over again. I assumed that this particular car was an example.

Just as I was about a half-block away, I heard a very loud bang! Turning around, I saw a great deal of smoke, parts of the car flung around, and the glass in the office window completely gone. Having no idea of what was occurring, I continued walking rapidly back to my own car, and then began driving back home to New London, Connecticut.

Checking *The New York Times* the next day, I found a story about a terrorist group called the Armenian Secret

Army, which claimed full responsibility for the bombing of that Turkish office. The particular unit involved, which termed itself the Yanikian Commandos, had joined other Armenian extremists in attacking Turkish targets in retaliation for the alleged genocidal murder of some million-and-a-half Turkish Armenians in the early decades of the 20th Century.

In particular, they demanded freedom for Gourgen Yanikian, an Armenian accused of murdering two Turkish diplomats. I then wrote an article for my local paper, *The New London Day*, describing the entire experience, titled 'A Close Brush With Terrorism'. *Terrorism* was a new term at that time, but one destined to become a watchword in the decades which have followed.

Given the time of the explosion, just after 5 p.m., had I stayed until the end of the meeting, it is highly probable that I would have been outside the Turkish Information Office just as that car blew up – taking me with it, most likely. Why I was internally pressed to leave a bit early remains the great mystery of this incident – but I always think about the references in many books to a still, small voice guiding many of us to our destinies. That voice was most assuredly with me on October 26, 1973, telling me that it was time to leave the meeting, and thus saving my life. I would like to believe that same voice is still with me today. In any event, this was my sixth miracle.

SEVEN

THE FUNERAL,
AND THE FRIEND

May 9, 1993
Forest Hills, New York

After the early death of my father at age 56, my mother
Anne continued to live at the family home in Kettering,
Ohio for some years. However, due to her not driving a
car, the suburbs were inconvenient. Further, widows were
looked upon with some distrust in Ohio, and there was
even a taint of husband-hunting, which caused formerly-
friendly couples to avoid socializing with unattached
women. After a few years, mother decided to move back
to New York City, where the remainder of the family was
located. She found a studio apartment on 63rd Drive in
Rego Park, remaining there for nearly thirty years until
her final illness.

Even though mother was eighty-nine years old when
she passed away, her death was still a shock. My family
and I had been living in Windsor, Connecticut for a dozen
years and visiting her regularly. It was only a three-hour
drive to Rego Park, at least on weekends when traffic was
endurable. Also, since I was Hartford regional manager

for a worldwide securities firm based in New York City, I could visit mother on trips to the head office, sometimes taking her back to Windsor to stay with us for a while before she went home to Rego Park.

In the mid-1980s, mother had taken a bad fall in the lobby outside her third floor apartment, when the elevator, after stopping, had failed to come level with the lobby floor, causing her to trip and hurt her legs and back. After that, her mobility was reduced, but she refused physical therapy. In place of her trips to neighborhood stores and markets, and a nearby department store called Alexanders, she set up a support network in which stores' staff came regularly to her apartment, bringing her everything she needed to survive, and even thrive, in Rego Park. Our family visits became stay-in affairs, rather than traveling to neighborhood restaurants. But, perhaps because I did not want to admit her growing feebleness, I accepted her preference that we bring meals to her, rather than taking her out to eat.

I had just returned from a local meeting early in May, 1993, when I was informed that mother had been taken by ambulance to a hospital in Kew Gardens, New York, after feeling sick and activating her Life Alert warning button in her apartment. For the next week, I moved into her apartment and spent as much time as possible at that hospital – but there was little hope, as the physicians said that she was far too weak to survive an operation for a strangulated intestine. On Friday, when I had to return home, I told mother that I would respect her decision as to whatever course she needed to pursue. Late that night, the hospital called me to confirm her demise, telling me that she had hung on longer than expected, waiting for my consent for her to leave. It was a sad moment, but we had said our goodbyes; and indeed, mortality is inherent in humanity.

In the Jewish tradition, funerals and burials take place

as soon as possible after a person dies, and there is an immediate seven-day period of mourning termed 'Shiva'. Mother's only immediate relatives were my own family, and as her only child, it fell to me to handle the details of her funeral on Sunday, May 9, 1993, which happened also to be Mother's Day that year. I had written a tribute to her, titled 'A Woman of Valor', which I would read at her funeral. Other family members, including my son Martin, would also express their thoughts. The entire family had been very fond of mother, also known as Grandma Anne to all of us. Being born in 1904, she had seen most of the 20th Century, and had shared her fascinating history with all of us.

The day before the funeral coincided with a final exam in Principles of Economics, which I had been teaching at Central Connecticut State University for some years, while serving as executive director of the local office of a worldwide securities firm. There was no possible way to re-schedule the exam, since it was due to start only a few hours after mother died, and at that time there were no email addresses available for students. My mother would have wanted me to carry out this final teaching duty, and I did so, but with a heavy heart. Then, heading home to Windsor, Connecticut from the University in New Britain, the motor in my Pontiac Fiero began to heat up, and its radiator was boiling as I neared home. At that point, I pulled into my local repair shop and asked what they would give for the car as it was. The owner replied that all he really wanted was the stereo radio.

Being distraught, all I wanted to do was to handle the necessary funeral arrangements. This was the second engine problem with the Fiero, and since it had a mid-engine, it was very hard to repair. The owner of the repair shop bought the car from me on the spot – and I walked home to get our other car and head to Forest Hills, New

York, where the funeral home used by my family for several generations was located. By mid-afternoon, all of the arrangements were made, including placing a death notice in the Sunday New York Times – a part of the pre-funeral procedure not explained to me in advance. The funeral home took care of that duty, and most of the other arrangements, as is customary.

My entire family, including all three sons, arrived at the Forest Hills funeral home around noon on Sunday, May 9. Upon being shown to the specific room where mother's funeral would take place, and after saying a final goodbye to mother, who lay in a traditional Jewish plain pine casket, we settled into chairs to wait for the funeral service to begin. As the 1 p.m. starting time approached, we were quite surprised as nearly a dozen men and women whom we did not know came into the room one-by-one and sat down in the rear. I got up and walked over to them, both to welcome them and also to ask about their connections to my mother. It turned out that she had led a double life of sorts, as each person there had helped to meet her needs, one way or another, so that she had not had to leave her studio apartment at all.

When we had visited, for the past five years or more, she always came up with an excuse to stay home, and we had avoided pressing her to go out to shop or eat. Instead, we either brought food with us, or picked up some meals in her busy neighborhood. Mother had kept the extent of her frailty from us to avoid upsetting us – but her postal carrier, delivery staff, tradespersons and neighbors had loved and cared for her, and all were now saying goodbye.

Then, just as the funeral service was about to start, one more person entered the room – a tall, distinguished middle-aged man who bore a strong resemblance to someone whom I had once known very well in the past, but had not seen for some thirty years: Peter Drew, my best friend from elementary and middle school in Jamaica, New York. I practically jumped out of my seat, running up to Peter and shaking hands with him. I asked how he had happened to know of mother's death, and he responded that he had seen the death notice which the funeral home had posted in The New York Times that very morning, and had been absolutely determined to pay his respects. He had known and remembered my mother and father, just as I had known his own mother decades before.

The last time I had seen Peter Drew had been when he visited our family in Brigantine, New Jersey in the late 1960s, during the period recounted earlier in this book. Although he remained in his native New York City, I had moved around the East and Midwest, and we had been out of touch for some twenty-five years. We did not have current addresses for each other, and our life situations had changed a great deal during that period. Still, we had never forgotten each other, or our early years together – and we have stayed in touch ever since 1993. My wife Birgit and I visited Peter and Deanna Drew in NYC in 2010, and were very pleased to see the couple well, happy, and enjoying life and many blessings. In the fall of 2015, Peter celebrated his 80th birthday at a special reception at the Metropolitan Museum of Art.

What is truly miraculous is how the death of a parent brought two friends together again after decades of separation, and how it took the unauthorized placement of a death notice by a funeral home to achieve that result. But it took even more than that: The New York Times publishes hundreds of such death notices on a daily basis, and the chances that one particular notice would be spotted by my best friend – and that he would be able to come to the funeral ceremony – are tiny, even virtually non-existent. I have always remained convinced that some force persuaded Peter Drew to spot that particular New York

Times item on that May 9, 1993 date, and have been further impressed that he was able to come to mother's funeral on such short notice.

Some might call this fate, or destiny, or mere happenstance – but for me, it was a true miracle, particularly since the sad loss of my mother had produced such a positive side effect. Mother would indeed have been very pleased, and perhaps she was. As the years have passed, and my friendship with Peter has been renewed, I think more and more often of that occurrence as an important part of the meaning of the funeral of my mother, and as my seventh miraculous event.

EIGHT
THE GOOD FENCE

July, 1994
Israel-Lebanon Border

Preamble

By way of background: The Good Fence (הבוטה רדגה) was a term that referred to Israel's mountainous 80-mile northern border with Lebanon during the period following the Lebanese Civil War and the 1978 South Lebanon conflict. At the time, southern Lebanon was controlled by the Maronite Christians and the South Lebanon Army.

From the 1948 establishment of the State of Israel until 1970, Israel's border with Lebanon was quiet to the point that farmers from the Israeli town of Metula farmed their lands in the Ayoun Valley inside Lebanon. In 1970, after their expulsion from Jordan during Black September, the PLO began taking control over southern Lebanon and breaking the tranquility that resided in the area.

The beginning of The Good Fence coincides with the beginning of the civil war in Lebanon in 1976 and the Israeli support of the Maronite Christians in southern Lebanon in their battle with the PLO. From 1977, Israel allowed the Maronites to find employment in Israel and helped them in exporting goods through the Israeli port city of Haifa. The main border crossing was the Fatima Gate near Metula.

Israel states that, before 2000, approximately one-third of the patients in the ophthalmology department of the Western Galilee Hospital were Lebanese citizens who crossed the border through the Good Fence and received treatment free of charge. The Good Fence ceased to exist with Israel's withdrawal from southern Lebanon in 2000. (Posting from Wikipedia, July 2016) My eighth miracle involves The Good Fence itself:

* * *

My first trip to Israel took place in July, 1978, thanks to my mother, who covered the costs of our entire family joining a Mission to Israel. It was one of the most memorable experiences of our lives. The historic Peace Agreement between Israel and Egypt was quite fresh, with American President Jimmy Carter playing a key role in the negotiations. Thus, Jimmy Carter kept a promise I had heard him make in Boston, while running for President, that he would actively foster peace in the Mid-east. His efforts resulted in a peace agreement negotiated between Israeli Prime Minister Menachem Begin and Egyptian President Anwar Sadat, and the return by Israel of the Sinai Peninsula to Egypt. Our trip included a visit to Israeli farmers in the Sinai region who were displaced as a result of the return of the entire Sinai to Egypt. Still, such adjustments are the price of peace – even if it turned out to be a somewhat-cold peace, it removed the largest Arab nation from active hostility and aggression towards Israel. That peace agreement worked.

Still, and regretfully, there have been no other comparable peace agreements between Israel and her Arab neighbors. Several times, such as in 1993, when U.S. President Bill Clinton tried to broker an agreement between Israel and the Palestinians, peace appeared close – but no agreement was achieved. These facts bring me to a later trip to the Mideast in July, 1994 – and to The Good Fence between Israel and its neighbor, Lebanon.

It has often been said that Lebanon, with its substantial Christian population, would be the second Middle East nation to make peace with Israel. The Good Fence, described above, is an indicator of that strong possibility – even though, unfortunately, it no longer exists as it did before 2000. My own visit to the Lebanese border, in the area near Metula, was prompted by remarks from a former American dentist who had emigrated to Israel years before and was now handling both routine and emergency dental problems in Jerusalem. This dentist pointed out that a significant number of his patients came from Arab nations, often under assumed identities and in Western dress, via The Good Fence on the Lebanese border. He stated that he had treated Saudi Arabian princes, Arab sheiks, Palestinians and their leaders, and many others who were official enemies of Israel, but were much more concerned with getting the best dental care than with pursuing national political issues.

Seeking to understand how the Good Fence worked, I arranged to visit the Israeli border with Lebanon near Metula, where the Fatima Gate admitted people from Lebanon and beyond into Israel. Several days later, my bus arrived in that vicinity, and I walked the rest of the way, through rugged terrain, to the border. My first impression was surprise at the minimal height of the fence, and its lack of barbed wire. It reminded me of the type of fence often found between the properties of reasonably friendly neighbors, used to show the demarcation lines between their properties. My second impression was to recall a line from a Robert Frost poem, Mending Fences: *Good Fences Make Good Neighbors.*

As I stood outside the rather narrow Fatima Gate, in the early evening of a warm July night, I noted a continuous and varied flow of people coming through from Southern Lebanon into Israel. Many wore Arab headgear and robes; some wore Western-style business suits; and some were dressed casually in jeans or shorts, and T-shirts. Entire families came through The Good Fence, along with individuals and couples. Their papers, particularly passports, were checked by Israeli soldiers stationed on the Israeli side of the gate. I did not see anyone rejected during the period of about a half hour while I watched the flow of humanity from Lebanon into Israel. The amazing, even miraculous, factor here was that these two nations officially remained enemies who were nominally at war – which did not seem to interfere in the slightest with that continuous inflow of humanity!

My tour guide, an academic from Hebrew University in Jerusalem, who earned extra income over the summer by leading such tours and who spoke impeccable English, described the details of the people coming through The Good Fence. They came from all over the Arab world. Not just from Lebanon, but also from Jordan, Saudi Arabia, and even from arch-enemy Iran, often on so-called 'special passports' which carried disguised identities. Some were even ruling officials of their nations, while others ranged from farmers to business leaders. Many. as noted above in the Wikipedia blurb on The Good Fence, were seeking medical care in Israel, which was unavailable in their home countries, and was normally rendered free-of-charge by Israeli hospitals and university medical staff as a goodwill gesture. I noticed a few children and adults with obvious handicaps or birth defects, as well as a substantial number of aged and infirm people hobbling along through the

Gate. Good dental care also turned out to be a high priority for some of those entrants.

Israeli diplomat, former Foreign Minister and United Nations Ambassador Abba Eban often stated that nations must make peace with their enemies, rather than with their friends, as peace between friendly nations is taken for granted. The wisdom of Abba Eban's view was proven at The Good Fence, as nearly all of those entering from Lebanon – or, in many cases, through Lebanon from other and less-friendly Arab nations – were official enemies of the State of Israel. They came from nations that had waged repeated wars against Israel – nations still vowing to push Israelis into the sea, and to reclaim all of the land that the United Nations had granted to create the State of Israel in 1948. {I recall one terrorist, around that same time, being asked why he killed Israeli children, after he had bombed a school bus on the beach near Tel Aviv. He replied that they grew up to become Israeli soldiers.}

In spite of all of that rhetoric and hatred, The Good Fence proved that it is possible for people to live in peace together, even when they come from hostile nations. For decades, an organization called Seeds of Peace has taken further steps and sought reconciliation and friendship between Israelis and their Palestinian neighbors, as well as with the Arab nations. The unexpected, surprising, and encouraging result at The Good Fence, of nominal enemies existing together in true peace – Shalom in Hebrew, Salaam in Arabic – is my eighth miracle. It has been a sign of hope for humanity. May there be more Good Fences in the future.

NINE
THE EPIPHANY

January 1, 2000
Bennington, Vermont

Preamble

Early in 1994, I had decided to leave my post as Con-
necticut-Western Massachusetts executive director for the
worldwide Development Corporation for Israel for several
reasons. First, I had been serving in that capacity for the
previous twelve years, all the while watching the work
become less and less satisfying due to major management
changes at our New York City national headquarters. This
trend had led to micromanagement of campaigns, and
even of our daily work. Second, because I was two-term
president of our professional staff union, the Association
of Professional Personnel, I had been denied promotion to
head our Boston office by supervisors whose limited vision
matched their limited ability. Third, though for several
years I had sought a comparable position at another firm,
I had found that being in my 50s was prohibitive in an
era when youth was a required job trait – and one which
I could not manage to acquire. Finally, the loss of my
mother provided some funds, which I decided to invest in

a socially-useful business, such as an old age home. Since it was too late to do more for her, the least I could do was to help others in their 80s and 90s to continue and be all that they could be – a very appropriate venture, particularly in view of the experience of my mother, and many other elderly persons, who lived alone and at risk for extended periods.

As I had found on occasion earlier in my life, chance or fate intervened again on a weekend in June, 1994, when I took a road trip in my Honda Del Sol to see a vintage automobile show in Southern Vermont, not far from the City of Bennington. Before touring the show, I hiked to the Appalachian Trail segment along Route 7 near Bennington, and then a short distance along the famous 2080-mile Trail from Maine to Georgia, as I hoped to hike at least a small part of the Appalachian Trail in every state that it traversed. This was my opportunity to add Vermont to the previous treks.

By the time I hiked back to my car, it was well past lunchtime and I was quite hungry, so I drove into Bennington and stopped at a small Chinese restaurant on Route 7. After ordering a spicy lunch, I found that I had left my book du jour in the Honda – and being a compulsive reader, I picked up a copy of the typical real estate brochure from a table in the restaurant, and started to flip through it. Then, one listing jumped out at me from its page: an old age home in Pownal, Vermont, a few miles South of Bennington, was on the market – and the price would be affordable for me if I could get a mortgage. I rushed to finish lunch, got directions to the Pownal realtor's office, and drove there at once, finding her at her desk and available to show me the property, and thereby changing my life forever!

Two months later, I had secured the needed mortgage, purchased the Victorian Pownal Community Care Home, and given notice to the Development Corporation for Israel that I would be leaving my executive post with them in late-September 1994 to run my new business venture. This was an exciting period, if not a financially rewarding one. A few years later, a major fire caused by a careless resident who had been smoking next to our building closed us down as an old age home – and my life shifted drastically once again.

After the fire, my facility could no longer be certified as a community-care home, without extensive renovations which were considerably beyond the insurance which we carried. I was able, however, to convert the property into a rooming house for various people in need of housing, including some on probation, provided by local law enforcement, and some with psychiatric problems, provided by the local counseling service. Meanwhile, since a rooming house could not generate sufficient income, I took on the task of Humane Investigator for the Bennington County Humane Society, handling cases of animal abuse, neglect, and cruelty. This half-time work came to mean a great deal to me, as I have always loved animals, and even as a child in New York City we had owned both dogs and cats.

Vermont takes responsible companion animal treatment very seriously, and I was proud to be responsible for enforcing the various laws, rules, and regulations in over 400 cases. The extensive training required to do so was also very useful; I became involved at the State of Vermont level and was appointed to ADEPT: Animals in Disasters Emergency Planning Team, which wrote the Vermont regulations for handling animals in such cases.

Meanwhile, time was passing, and the new Century and Millennium were approaching. (Now, I must add another dimension to My Many Miracles by writing on a more-personal level. Previously, my personal life was not so germane to the miracles that had occurred – but that situation changed forever as the Year 2000 neared.) Nor was I alone regarding the impact of such changes, leading to a new designation for the event: Y2K, a time of both hope and dread, ranging from those who believed in the Second Coming of the Savior to those who thought all computers and computer systems would be irreparably damaged by the changed digit at the start of Year 2000. My own change was different, but indeed it led to my ninth miraculous event:

* * *

Bennington, Vermont – the city nearest Pownal – where my then-wife and I resided – had joined the popular First Night practice of staging, for one nominal fee, a wide variety of public New Year's Eve events and activities, in order to welcome the New Year safely, sanely, and enjoyably. In the early 1990s, we had participated in First Nights in Hartford, Connecticut, which were quite elaborate and included free bus service to and from the city until 3 a.m. on each January 1. So, we were ready to try the Bennington version of First Night on December 31, 1999, to welcome the new Century and Millennium in style.

After making the rounds of programs held all over Bennington, mostly within walking distance of each other, we ended the evening in a large local church, where the entire First Night audience could join in the count-down to January 1, 2000. That was when my miraculous epiphany occurred, changing my life and future profoundly and irrevocably.

As the final ten seconds of 1999 were counted down by the audience, based on a large clock at the front of the church on which seconds were prominently displayed, time seemed to freeze for me. The subjective gap from second to second became longer and longer, while a thought was repeated over and over inside my head. That thought was as follows: *I absolutely needed to make some major changes in my life in 2000; I absolutely needed to do something very different from what I had been doing; I absolutely needed to become someone different, too.* As the final second of 1999 became the very first second of 2000, I vowed to follow the advice I had been given, despite not knowing its source or ultimate impact. Frankly, there was little choice in making my decision: this was a true and major epiphany for me.

I did not share this epiphany with my then-wife, a proud atheist who would likely have mocked me for it. Also, at that point I had no idea of the nature of the changes I needed to make in my life – the epiphany had not been that specific, and I needed to think about it to achieve a better understanding. Still, I had no slightest doubt that a message had been sent to me, from somewhere and something outside of myself. Having taken some courses in psychology, I understood the concept of projection, examining the possibility that this epiphany was really the result of wishful thinking on my part. But, after weeks of reflection, I could not accept that analysis, which implied that I was dissatisfied with my present life and was merely finding an excuse to change it. In truth, I had been quite happy, even if our marriage was not a warm one, something which I had come to accept.

I loved scenic and progressive Vermont; I loved my humane investigative work; I loved my volunteer duties as Pownal emergency management coordinator; and I even loved some extra tasks which I had undertaken as part-time advance staff for the massive United States Census 2000 program, the goal of which was to count and record each American resident, as required every ten years by our Constitution. Why should I make major changes to what appeared to be working for me? I even recalled that old adage: If something is not broken, do not try to fix it. Yet, despite all that, I could not quite get over my Y2K epiphany.

It took several more months for the nature of the changes that I needed to make in my life to become clear. There was a gradual process in which I thought about the epiphany and compared its impact to my day-to-day life, analyzing the positive and negative sides. A Spring 2000 trip to visit my brother-in-law in the North Georgia mountains solidified my conclusions, due to some incidents that shed light on my actual marital situation. It became increasingly clear that my marriage was at the root of my dissatisfaction. Nor did I believe that the marriage was doing much for my then-wife, either. It was time for both of us to move on in our lives. Still, that realization was a rather painful one, as we had been married at the time for thirty-two years, had had a son together; and I had two step-children, all of whom I loved dearly. What, as it turned out, I did not love, was our own marital situation, which was never going to improve beyond its present lukewarm state.

By May of 2000, the Rubicon resulting from my epiphany was crossed, and my decision was indeed made. During that month, I asked my then-wife for a divorce, to which she agreed. We proceeded in as cooperative a fashion as possible via a negotiated settlement.

In December of that year, after the mandatory Vermont six-month waiting period elapsed, a reasonably friendly divorce was granted, and each of us could then move on with our lives. For me, there was a vast sense of relief that at least the divorce process had ended.

My New Year 2000 epiphany had resulted in a drastic change in our lives, which turned out to be for the better for both of us. The form and content of the epiphany were truly miraculous in nature, even if its source remains mysterious to this very day. Had I not trusted in the insight provided by that epiphany, my life would have continued in the same old, tired mode.

Further, this event led to several other miraculous events, which are described in the remainder of *My Many Miracles*. It would seem that miracles can build upon one another, a chain reaction seemingly unexplained – and perhaps unexplainable – rationally. Regardless, this Y2K epiphany – and its outcome – became my ninth miracle.

TEN

NEW HOUSE – NEW SPOUSE

June 10, 2001
Hillsborough, New Hampshire

Preamble

Being a newly single man in his early 60s proved a
rather-difficult role to assume. The dating scene was
vastly different from what little I recalled after a lapse of
more than thirty years, and this was not only due to the
emergence of computer dating websites, none of which I
was prepared to join. Instead, I became involved in area
activities in the tri-state region of Southern Vermont,
Northern Massachusetts, and Eastern New York. There
were numerous groups promoting animal welfare, aiding
the elderly, and seeking civic betterment in my area, and I
became involved with a number of them – leading me to
meet eligible women, some of whom I dated.

Several bizarre and unpleasant experiences resulted
from my efforts, however. Once, I traveled over an hour
to Albany, New York, to meet a nurse who proceeded to
lecture me against dating while I was only legally separated
but not yet fully divorced. Then, a woman who had moved
from Montana to be with her daughter in Vermont, and

who had then prepared a lovely dinner-for-two, suddenly dropped me like a hot potato for no apparent reason. So I began to use the computer to seek compatible dates, which mainly produced endless email correspondences with lonely ladies, but little else. There was also a substantial amount of misinformation provided by some of those engaging in computer dating, and even risk that a possible partner had ulterior motives. The few ongoing relationships that emerged ended up being flawed, and I despaired.

Meanwhile, I had been offered a hazard mitigation consultancy by the New Hampshire Office of Emergency Management, stemming from volunteer emergency management work as coordinator for the Town of Pownal, Vermont, which in turn led to regional and statewide activities such as service on the Local Emergency Preparedness Committee for Bennington County, and on ADEPT – the Animals in Disasters Emergency Planning Team, which wrote the official Vermont document on this topic. I had also been trained by FEMA, the Federal Emergency Management Agency – so now I had a part-time job in nearby New Hampshire!

What I did not have, though, was a regular place to reside from Mondays to Fridays, when I needed to be near Concord, New Hampshire, in order to handle my duties of closing out some forty-three open emergency management hazard mitigation projects around that state. On weekends, I continued to live in the former Pownal Community Care Home, even with its fire damage, which did not prevent the use of much of the property. On weekdays I lived in my large Southwind RV, with my two dogs, Tucker and Domino, at a campground in Epsom, NH.

In April of 2001, just as my split-living arrangements appeared to be working smoothly, I got an unpleasant surprise from the owner-operator of the quality Circle 9 campground where my RV had been located since the previous year. There was a notice posted on the windshield of my RV one day when I returned from my job at Emergency Management. It stated that so-called Spring and Summer monthly rental rates were going into effect in May of 2001, since the demand for RV campsites was seasonal and the season of heavy usage was nearly upon us – in fact, my monthly rental was going to triple (the new figure was written in a blank space left on the notification form). I had to either pay the tripled monthly rental fee or leave the campground by the end of that month. Neither choice was desirable, nor even acceptable due to the short notice time being given to me.

Immediately, I went to see the campground owner and asked for an extension for at least two months of the present rate that I had been paying. This was granted, as I had been a good and trouble-free renter. That extension provided some more time for me to chase a dream that I had had ever since living on the Brigantine Inland Waterway in New Jersey in the late 1960s. I hoped to find a house on a lake or river near Concord.

The former Pownal Community Care Home had been on the market ever since its major fire several years before, and there were starting to be some nibbles from possible buyers. Perhaps the tripling of the monthly rental for my RV campground spot was a blessing in disguise, as now I was being forced to find more permanent housing – hopefully on some body of water, if I were really lucky! My top priority became the search for such housing.

Unfortunately, though, my search for waterfront housing produced little success for some six weeks, as I checked the Concord Monitor newspaper real estate listings and the MLS realtor listings regularly but found nothing affordable on a lake or river. Spring is the hot real estate season in New Hampshire, once the snows of winter have melted and more and more properties are being bought up by people from the Boston and New York areas. I had pretty much given up on finding any property meeting my criteria, and thus having to pay the tripled campground rental fee until I could move to an apartment, unless some other option emerged.

Then, on the morning of June 10, 2001, I opened the Concord Monitor to the real estate classified listings – and one jumped out at me immediately: a ranch home on Emerald Lake in Hillsborough, New Hampshire had just been reduced substantially to promote a quick sale. I called the listed realtor at once and made an appointment to see the lake house that very day, finding that it needed some work but was well worth its modest asking price. Emerald Lake was a lovely small lake only a half hour from my hazard mitigation work based in Concord. I offered the asking price on the spot. The realtor called the owners and my offer was immediately accepted. Since the house had been used as a summer home and was vacant, I moved my RV to it over the next weekend, then moved furniture from the fire-damaged community care home in Vermont – and for the second time in my life, I owned a home on the water: a dream achieved.

* * *

But all of that is only half of the story of events on June 10, 2001, as I found more than a new home that day. Coincidentally – or miraculously, if one prefers – I also found the love of my life on that same exact day. In addition to working for New Hampshire emergency management half-time, I had begun teaching economics and business courses several years before at Plymouth State University in Plymouth, New Hampshire, about an hour's drive North of Concord on Interstate 93. My part-time teaching included some student advising, which in turn led me to involvement with students who planned on transferring from Plymouth to the flagship University of New Hampshire in Durham, usually in order to complete their junior and senior years at UNH. On occasion, I would deal with the UNH department which handled student aid and grants.

One of my advisees planned on transferring to UNH for the Fall, 2001 semester, but some paperwork was not in order, and I had to discuss that problem with someone in the UNH student financial aid section. On my way back to Concord from Hillsborough, where I had made the accepted offer for the lake house there, I called UNH and spoke with a woman in financial aid who had a very nice voice and manner, and who really cared about facilitating student needs and solving financial problems. I complimented my new contact on her caring manner, and she complimented me for being a truly concerned teacher and advisor. After all of that mutual admiration, I discovered that she was undergoing a divorce – and I could commiserate with her, having recently gone through that process myself. I began to think that it would be nice to commiserate in person.

We arranged to meet for lunch in Portsmouth, New Hampshire the following week, as I had an emergency management project to review near there, only a short distance from Durham where my new contact worked. We met for lunch at the Stockpot Restaurant in Portsmouth during the second week of June, 2001 – and the rest is history. We continued to meet, her divorce was finalized, and we were married at Dover City Hall on December 20 of 2002. It seems miraculous that I found both a house, and a spouse – my wife Birgit – on the exact same day. We always celebrate each June 10, a very special anniversary date, as a reminder that miracles do happen, even to us ordinary people. This was, indeed, my tenth miracle.

ELEVEN
TUCKER AND THE BONE

September, 2004
Hillsborough, New Hampshire

Preamble

One of the outcomes of my work as Humane Investigator for the Bennington County (Vermont) Humane Society, which later became the Second Chance Animal Center, was my tendency to take, as companion animals, some of the dogs and cats which I collected through my duties. They had often been abandoned when their owners moved, or had been brought to the Humane Society by more-responsible owners who could no longer care for them. I tended to take the tough cases – dogs and cats which otherwise were unlikely to find homes, because they were old or sick or badly behaved, or just plain unattractive. In one instance, for example, a family called me because their patriarch had just died and they could not stand to see his Norwegian Elkhound around the house anymore, as a continual reminder of their loss. I was asked to pick up the dog during the funeral of its owner, so that they would not even have to see it being taken away. The Bear, as this dog was named, became part of my animal family, which reached a peak count of nearly twenty. It seemed only fitting that I should devote my modest earnings as Humane Investigator to the cause of helping animals who were otherwise very likely to be euthanized.

After accepting an out-of-Vermont job, which required me to live in my Southwind RV during weekdays, it was impossible for me to keep such a horde of companion animals. My ex-wife graciously consented to continue keeping most of the horde, or herd, at our former family home in Pownal, Vermont, and I happily agreed to pay half of their food and veterinary costs. Then came the painful decision as to which animals to choose to share my new RV lifestyle, and I decided that I should be able to handle two dogs. Cats were not feasible, as all of them tended to roam, which was not permissible in the RV park. More than two dogs would not be feasible in an RV either. And so, I chose my two favorites, Tucker and Domino – leading to the strange event that followed, and to my eleventh miracle.

* * *

Tucker and Domino were both rescued dogs via the Bennington County Humane Society. Tucker, a foxhound who looked like a long-legged beagle, was the very first dog I took as a companion animal after becoming the BCHS Investigative Agent. He had already been at the humane society for close to the maximum time allowed before becoming a likely candidate for euthanasia, as he was a bit unruly, tending to jump up on visitors, being difficult to walk, and generally unwilling to follow what BCHS considered proper canine rules of conduct. Still, the very first time he looked at me from his cage, with his big brown eyes full of love and longing for freedom, I was hooked – and Tucker went home with me!

Domino was rescued by me after a landlord told me

that the dog's owners had split suddenly without paying their monthly rent, leaving most of their possessions behind – including Domino, who was half Rottweiler and half Dalmatian, with a Rottie body and almost no tail, along with the classic Dalmatian black-on-white spots all over his body, and with one black eye and one white eye. I found him tied up at his former home, and was a bit worried about freeing him, as both of his breeds have a reputation for being difficult. But as he waggled his stumpy tail, I could see that he was a very sweet dog, and so Domino, named for his appearance, also went home with me. After my divorce, these two dogs became my canines-of-choice, living with me on weekends in the fire-damaged former care home, and weekdays in my Southwind RV at Circle 9 Campground in Epsom, New Hampshire.

When my son Martin learned that I had become engaged to Birgit, in 2001, his comment was that, while she might accept me provisionally, she was unlikely to be willing to take on Tucker and Domino. However, Birgit had been a lover of companion animals for her entire life, and she came to love these two canines just as much as I did. While Domino proved to be one of the best dogs in the world, with no bad habits at all, Tucker always found a way to be difficult – as when he jumped up with his front paws on a kitchen counter and lifted a T-bone steak we had been saving for a special occasion, and which we were unable to get him to drop. As matters turned out, though, we did not end up begrudging that steak to Tucker, as we learned shortly afterwards that he was quite ill, and this was one of his last thefts.

We went to Cape Cod in Massachusetts every year, often over the Winter Holidays when there was beautiful new snow on the ground and a wild ocean to view. The last time we took Tucker with us, along with Domino, he showed little spirit for running on the beach. We thought he was just a bit off-stride, so we took him to the veterinarian upon our return, and started giving him some pep-up pills. But as far as we knew at first, his lethargy was nothing serious – until his condition worsened. Tucker became more and more lethargic, and it was a struggle to get him to walk on a leash near our weekday duplex in Farmington, New Hampshire, where we had moved after being married in 2002. After further trips to our veterinarian, he was diagnosed with a serious condition involving some form of malignancy, which we tried unsuccessfully to treat. Tucker died peacefully at home in the Spring of 2004. We carried him from Farmington to our house at Emerald Lake in Hillsborough, to bury him there, all the while mourning the loss of our fond companion.

That burial was indeed a sad duty, and it was a sad period for both of us. Tucker had been about eight years old when he died, and he had been my companion animal for over six years. Birgit had come to love him also, and we had accepted his strong-willed nature as normal for him. Domino clearly missed his companion too, and moped around both the Farmington duplex and our weekend house in Hillsborough. Given the relatively short canine lifespan, it was not unusual to lose a companion animal – but Tucker had always been special, and each of us felt he should have lived longer than he did. Our grieving process just did not seem to end, in the case of the loss of Tucker. Then, what seemed like a miracle occurred.

I had put all of the items associated with Tucker, such as his collar and leash, in a box, which I saved as mementos of his period living with us. His dog licenses were included, and perhaps it seems morbid to have saved such items, but they meant a great deal to me. However, there was a special nylon bone we had gotten for Tucker from our veterinarian as a tooth strengthener as well as a toy, which I had been unable to find after Tucker died. I had assumed it was under some piece of furniture and would turn up eventually – and so it did, but not in any way which I might have anticipated.

On a fine late September weekend day in 2004, nearly half a year after we lost Tucker, I was raking leaves in the driveway at our lake house in Hillsborough, NH. As I moved up the driveway towards Hemlock Street, on which our house was situated, I saw a flash of something white and about eight inches long under the leaves – something which had not been there before those leaves fell, as I would have noticed any items on a bare driveway.

There, on top of the leaves, was Tucker's nylon bone, complete with his embedded tooth marks. It had not been there the night before when we pulled our Chevrolet Blazer into the driveway, or it would have shown up clearly in the headlights as it was not buried. It was just there, very visible, as if Tucker had dropped it very recently – which was totally impossible, as Tucker had been buried just a few yards away, under an oak tree and with a wooden marker.

I picked up the nylon bone and examined it. It was clearly Tucker's property, as we had bought a similar bone for Domino that was inside our house, where Domino had dropped it. The bone I found had not been there the night before, nor even that morning when I had gone outside to check the weather. My conclusion was that some force had arranged for us to find the bone, as a way of saying that all was well with Tucker and that we should get on with our lives; we should remember Tucker fondly, but not dwell on his loss. I have no other explanation. I do, however, still have the nylon bone in the same box with Tucker's other items; and to this very day, I do still consider this to be my eleventh miracle. It is very gratifying to think that miracles may sometimes involve beloved companion animals, like Tucker.

TWELVE
THE GATEWAY TO THE GODS

June, 2010
Delphi, Greece

Preamble

My first visit to Greece took place in the summer of 1961 as part of a European trip with my friends Robert W. Kuhns, Jr. (the same Bob Kuhns previously discussed in Section 3 of this book) and Pat Moran, who worked at Gem City Savings Bank in Dayton, Ohio. We flew from Dayton to Germany, rented a small Mercedes in Nuremberg, and after touring the former Yugoslavia, we drove down through Northern Greece, ending up in Athens. That visit to Greece was among the most memorable parts of a very memorable journey, and I had expected to return in 1963 to complete my doctorate in economics at the econometric institute in Athens headed by Andreas Papandreou, who later became prime minister of Greece – a post eventually won by his son, George Papandreou. But the untimely death of my father in late 1962 intervened, and I was unable to return then. Still, Greece, a major source of Western civilization, has always held special meaning for me.

Thus, ever since finding my wife Birgit and living part

of each year in Sweden, Greece had been high on our list of European countries to visit. Birgit and I were fascinated by all of the Western history, philosophy, literature, and even science that had originated in Ancient Greece. I was also quite interested in the Greek economic model, which has had serious issues. In June of 2010, we were able to plan a trip to Greece from our home on the island of Gotland, Sweden. We arranged to visit Athens for a few days, focusing on such monuments as the Acropolis and ancient churches, as well as the ebullient life of the city itself. We then planned to take a ferry to at least one Greek island in the Aegean Sea; and also to make a visit to Delphi, home of the ancient Oracle and many ruins and historical sites, by bus from Athens. All of this touring was feasible without having to rent a car, and we were looking forward to sampling Greek public transport.

As matters turned out, however, the experience became less than satisfying when my U.S. passport and some euros were stolen from my buttoned shorts pocket on the Greek Metro, which we tried to take to get to the departure point for the bus to Delphi. I was the victim of a classic pick-pocket technique where one man blocks the victim from moving while another deftly lifts the flap on the pocket and takes the goods. Birgit was the first to notice the open pocket, and we got off the Metro at the next stop to report the theft to the Athens Police. We discovered that dealing with those worthies was far worse than being a pickpocket victim. The police refused to let me call the theft a theft, demanding that I sign a form stating that I had merely lost my items, which would make their statistics look better. Upon refusing to lie for them, we were put into a room with a number of criminal suspects and left to cool our heels. But we persisted.

Finally, after missing the opportunity to catch the bus to Delphi, I was allowed to sign a form in Greek, upon night in Greece before returning to our home in Gotland, Sweden. It had been a wonderful visit, and even more wonderful was that I found the lump had continued to get smaller even before we left Greece. Over the next few days, in Sweden, it disappeared completely, as did the itching sensation and all pain! It has never returned, and it seems that my prayers in Delphi cured me of a very painful and dangerous condition. Upon returning to America, months later, that cure was confirmed by my family doctor, who withdrew a call for me to see a specialist.

Undoubtedly, many people will give many explanations for this miraculous occurrence. I have no explanation for it, beyond what has been written here. Whether my childhood interest in the ancient gods produced a modern-day medical miracle is indeed speculative. The reader may draw his or her own conclusions as to the exact cause and nature of this event – but that the event occurred is not in doubt, nor is the confirmation by Birgit that an opening or cave emerged on once-sacred Mount Parnassus which had not been there before. This is, therefore, my twelfth miracle, and probably the most unexplainable of all those covered in this book.

* * *

Perhaps, though, this will not be the final miracle of my life. At eighty years of age, a continuing healthy life seems like a miracle of sorts itself, each and every day. Finding true love after so many years, and being privileged to live in two great nations on two different continents, are things which I would never have expected to happen. Being able to write a series of books in different genres, including four books of poetry, a self-help book, and endless Op Eds, would never have occurred to me until I sat down and started writing some fifteen years ago.

There may well be more miraculous events waiting, not only for Birgit and me, but for all of us. We need only have the will to seek them out, the senses to find them, and the heart to recognize miracles when they occur. All life is mysterious, and miraculous as well. It is surely worth the time and effort to understand, and act upon, those truths.

ADDENDUM:
MY MISSING MIRACLE
A DRIVE ON THE WILD SIDE

Winter, 1996
Along Interstate 93 in Vermont, USA

Preamble

While writing *My Many Miracles: A Spiritual Journey*, I had considered including the following strange event – but I delayed a decision until after the remainder of the book was finished, as I was uncertain about whether to include it. This uncertainty stemmed from several factors: first, details as to exact timing of the event are not quite as firm as are those for the other miracles; second, the occurrence was the result of an unwise decision on my part, and hence a bit embarrassing; finally, the event resulted in actions covered in this addendum which might once have been considered confidential. Upon reflection, though, I have decided that what follows is a truly miraculous event, accurately described – and therefore deserves inclusion here.

* * *

A few months after taking charge of the Pownal Community Care Home in Vermont in the Fall of 1994, our facility joined the Vermont Health Care Association, our professional body. I had hoped this step would result in more residents for our own Home, as many VHCA nursing homes offered higher levels of care; when some resident's condition improved, that person might be switched over to a Community Home like ours. {Actually, I learned this rarely happened – nursing homes prefer to retain their residents' higher fees, rather than to send them elsewhere.}

Not knowing of that reality, however, I became active in the VHCA and was assigned the task of representing Residential Care Homes such as my own. This task required attendance at the monthly VHCA Board meetings, where I would make reports and answer questions. The Board met, usually on Tuesday afternoons, at VHCA Headquarters on Moonlight Terrace in Montpelier, Vermont, some three hours away by car from my Pownal Community Care Home.

Early in 1996, I was working with a troubled community care home, to help improve its performance – before the State of Vermont stepped in and possibly even closed the facility. It was State policy to allow the VHCA an opportunity to resolve problems before official action occurred. Our monthly VHCA Board meeting was scheduled for 1 p.m. on a Tuesday afternoon, as usual, and I was scheduled to give a report on the status of the problem facility. I left our own Pownal Community Care Home around 9 a.m. that morning for the three-hour drive to the meeting in Montpelier, the State capital, allowing an extra hour for my favorite "stop along the way" – lunch at the Ponderosa Restaurant in Rutland, directly on my way to the meeting. Ponderosa featured an "endless buffet" including many main courses, side dishes, appetizers, desserts, and drinks, all for under ten dollars per person. I fully intended to "pig out" – and I did, finishing around 11 a.m.

Continuing my drive North from Rutland, to pick up Interstate 93 towards Montpelier, I began to feel sleepy from all that lunch. I pulled off the road at a typical Vermont country store and got a cup of coffee, sitting in my small Honda Del Sol car for ten minutes to rest up and drink it. Then I reached I 93 and headed North again – but I still felt sleepy. I thought that I should pull over again and even take a brief nap, but snow had fallen the night before and the road was wet and a bit slippery. By then I was only a few miles away from my destination; in fact, I saw a sign reading *MONTPELIER: 8 MILES* – surely I could make it that far, and not be late for the meeting.

The very next thing that I knew, my two right-side wheels were off the road, on gravel with a coating of snow, making a grinding noise – and my Honda was heading over the edge of the road, towards a sharp drop-off to the Connecticut River hundreds of feet below. I fought the steering, managed to get all four wheels back on the main part of the highway, and then felt a sense of terror I had rarely felt previously in my entire life. I was shaking, and managed to pull off the road in the marked zone for the next exit, as I tried to recover from nearly having a fatal accident. Indeed, I had fallen asleep-at-the-wheel for the first time in my life!

Then, I looked up at the sign for this exit, which read: *MONTEPLIER: 1 MILE!* **It was my regular exit, and I had driven seven miles asleep-at-the-wheel, in a car on cruise control which maintained a cruising speed of 65 miles (100 kilometers) per hour!** I knew that this was a very close call – and, in central Vermont's mountains, likely a fatal one. There were steep drop-offs for most of the seven miles, as I knew this stretch of highway quite well from previous trips.

I thought about turning around and just heading home, as I did not feel up to attending a meeting, let alone giving a report. But that would have been embarrassing, and also would have meant a long drive with no rest. So, I slowly entered the exit and drove to the meeting, where I gave my report, listened to the other business, and managed to drive home after a lot more coffee.

On that drive home, I came to two decisions. One was to no longer have giant lunches at Ponderosa in Rutland, followed by a long drive. The other was to fight the trend for nursing homes to hold onto residents who no longer needed such a high level of care. I pressed that issue with Vermont authorities – but I never mentioned that it was the result of a **miraculous drive on the wild side!**

AFTERWORD:
A PHILOSOPHICAL VIEW OF
THE SOURCES OF MIRACLES

The reader may have noted that previously in this book, little has been written about the source or sources of miracles. That omission is intentional, for several reasons. In my view, it is quite presumptuous for any author to assert much about such matters, although such assertions are indeed often made. Further, as noted in the second part of the title of this book, it focuses on a spiritual journey, rather than on a religious journey per se. That focus is also intentional, as miracles seem to me to be part of all spiritual belief systems, rather than being limited to only one religion.

Recently, however, through the book Upasana: In the Presence of the Divine, which was loaned to me by my sister-in-law Barbro Klausner, I discovered the views of the two Swami Saraswatis of India, and I was particularly struck by one major point: a contrast between views of God in the Western and Eastern traditions. **Western religious tradition most typically asserts that God created the universe, whereas Eastern religious tradition states that God is the universe.** The distinction between these two views is crucial to spirituality as well as to religion

– yet I had been unaware previously of that important distinction, which also affects my views as to the sources of miracles.

If a Supreme Being created the universe – now expanded to the multiverse – then we must postulate that Supreme Being as its creator, and therefore some type of time must have existed before its creation occurred. These postulates are hard to grasp – and, to more and more humans, also difficult to accept. But there is no difficulty grasping the concept of the universe itself, or even of the multiverse – nor does it make much sense to challenge the obvious existence of either. Observation proves the universe, and higher mathematics proves the multiverse. By the Eastern tradition, then, God must – and does – exist, just as the universe or multiverse exists, for they are one and the same.

If God must exist, and if miracles do exist, it still does not follow that the first is necessarily the source of the second. Yet, those many miracles, which appear to be unexplainable by any ordinary means, and our logic, must of necessity have some other source. It would be presumptuous for any author to attempt to define that source specifically, but this author believes that at least some of those unexplainable and mysterious events have such a profound, unexplainable, and mysterious source.

The Swami Satyananda Saraswati writes in Upasana, page 140, that: *You have to be a light unto yourself… For God's grace, you do not have to qualify yourself… Always remember that God is never far from you.* Nor are miracles ever far from us, if we seek for them. We are all children of the universe, or of the multiverse, as the case may be. Let us then listen for that still, small voice inside us, and seek our own miracles. By finding them, ultimately we can find ourselves.

My very best wishes for your own quest!
Eugene F. Elander; Hollywood Hills, California

www.ingramcontent.com/pod-product-compliance
Lightning Source LLC
Chambersburg PA
CBHW071834020426
42331CB00007B/1721